There Is Something About The Icelandic Horse
ISBN: 9798735314516

Photographed and authored by Elisabeth Haug

Contact Elisabeth at Info@Ehaug.com
Pathfinder Publications
2585 Jacaranda Lane,
Los Osos, Ca 93402

Check out my website at https://SharingMagicMoments.com, https://EHaug.com, and https://ElisabethHaug.com.

There Is
Something About
The Icelandic Horse

MAY THE HORSE BE WITH YOU!

“There is no more sagacious animal than the Icelandic horse. He is stopped by neither snow, nor storm, nor impassable roads, nor rocks, glaciers, or anything. He is courageous, sober, and surefooted. He never makes a false step, never shies. If there is a river or fjord to cross (and we shall meet with many) you will see him plunge in at once, just as if he were amphibious, and gain the opposite bank.”

— Jules Verne, Journey to the Center of the Earth

On one of the seven occasions our Icelandic Horse group was selected to participate in the Rose Parade and we rode down Colorado Boulevard watched by 1.6 million people in person and 160 million people on television, the famous TV commentator and horseman—Bob Eubanks—announced the truest words I have ever heard about our Icelandic Horse.

"THE ICELANDIC HORSE IS MORE THAN A HORSE. HE IS A FRIEND!"

The horse has always been an integral part of Icelandic culture. Chances are that no other country in the world has a higher horse per capita ratio than this magical island. There is reason for that. To know the Icelandic Horse is to love him—not with a short-lived infatuation but with a life long passion. There are many things about him that makes him special—his courage; his street smarts; his endurance, strength and powerful motion; his light and sure feet; his smooth gaits; and most of all his kind, gentle, giving, co-operative, no nonsense, unpretentious, and friendly nature.

Come From
Your Heart

Every Breed Of Horse Is The Direct Result Of The Needs And Desires Of The Culture That Has Created It

The Icelandic Horse of today is the result of a long, ongoing saga. Over time, we have been told that it all began when the first Viking settlers brought their families, livestock, and chattel with them to Iceland about 1100 years ago. They sailed into the unknown in open Viking ships, braving the dangerous seas and steering only by the stars. The horses were tied in a long line to a boom stretching from the fore to the aft of the boat.

Whereas all this did happen, DNA research now reveals that the Icelandic Horse and the Mongolian Horse share some DNA. One can only speculate about how this interchange has occurred. But my guess would be that—way before Genghis Kahn—Mongolian traders brought herds of horses with them on the long, difficult way to Scandinavia. Chances are that the Vikings bought horses from the merchants among other goods.

This could explain how the Vikings' horses were able to transition easily to life in Iceland. They would already be bred and used to being tied together in groups of fifty or more while carrying burdens across the endless, rugged terrain in all kinds of weather. As such, it would be no problem for them to adjust to the harsh life in Iceland

Without their wonderful horses, it would not have been possible for the settlers to inhabit their island and thrive. Not only was a very special horse needed to cover their transportation needs, but he also became their major food supply.

Cattle needed to be stabled year-round. Sheep had to be fed hay and stabled during fall and winter. But the horses were able to fend for themselves on the range all year by scraping away the snow and eating the frozen grass underneath.

Whereas some may not like to think about the 90% of horses that intil recently were slaughtered every year in Iceland. The practice was necessary for human survival. Also—as a fringe benefit—the scenario is responsible for a much stricter selection within the Icelandic Horse than any other breed has experienced.

Even today, Icelandic Horses have several characteristics that are different from those of other breeds. They have a cannon bone shortening that gives them a lower center of gravity, increasing both their balance and their weight bearing capacity. It is this—along with the extra flexibility in their fetlock joints—that enable them to travel safely at high speeds across tufts and tussocks and other rough terrain. Their digestive system is also unique. Their coat is thermal, and unlike horses of other breeds they are able to pant like dogs in order to get rid of excess heat.

Life was harsh in Iceland and very dependent on weather. There was considerable work to do in the short times of good weather, and it was important to make the process as efficient as possible.

SYNERGY!

The breeding program the farmers used for their horses was simple, yet very effective. Only geldings were ridden. Mares were used solely for reproduction. All male foals were slaughtered except for the choice few selected to—down the line—replace the current favorite riding horses.

As a two or three year olds, the chosen stud colts were turned out—one at a time—with a herd of mares—either belonging to their owner or one of the neighbors. Once they had done the job, they were gelded and left to roam the range until it was time for their training to be started at four.

It was a simple and effective method, creating neither muss nor fuss. Furthermore—if the best colts for riding had been selected—the shorter generations caused by young stallions guaranteed a faster improvement of the overall herd.

Whenever their owners went on journeys to town, to family, or to friends, the young geldings were taken along as a part of the loose herd. Later, when they were four, they were brought in for their training to begin. They were hand-horsed for at least a year before being ridden, allowing them to become accustomed to the normal workflow.

The Black Stallion!

As a rule, unexperienced horses were tied to a surcingle tied around the belly of the horse actually being hand-horsed by the rider. This created a no argument situation and the young horse learned the tricks of the trade taught by more experienced horses rather than the rider. It was not uncommon for up to 5 horses to be tied together this way. By the time the horse was five and ready to ride, he knew what was expected of him and little actual training was needed.

Except for the rides to church on Sundays, only men and children rode around the farm. The women were too busy inside taking care of the extremely important household needs. However, farmers brought their families along on journeys to friends and family in other parts of the country. Plenty of fresh horses were brought along in a loose herd and frequent stops were made along the way to change horses, and to let the animals eat and urinate. The loose herds were also an opportunity for farmers across the country to exchange horses. When needed, you just found some neighbor or other person headed in the right direction and added your horse to their loose herd. Reehts' (corrals) where the horses could be enclosed were placed conveniently along the main trail for use by the public.

The horses were also taught to travel while tied head to tail in lines up to fifty or more swift moving horses. This was how the mail was delivered and the hay brought in.

Iceland has always been a nation of artists with a keen eye for beauty of every kind. Although the work contribution of the horses was an essential part of human survival and their labor was what was necessary for the Icelanders, there was also opportunity for a certain amount of rivalry. Who had the most beautiful, well moving, spectacular horses on Sundays when they rode to church, was a matter of prestige and as such important, too.

Time obviously did not stand still in Iceland, but for a long time nothing changed the importance of the horse. Unlike in so many other breeds, the riders needed independent, street smart horses who could make their own quick decisions. They had to bond with their mounts and trust their competence rather than direct their every step and discipline them.

All time favorites are the tales of how the horses were able to gauge the intoxication levels of their masters. On those occasions when the men gathered to socialize, the horses would carefully make their way home afterwards. They would balance in such a way as to keep their riders in the saddle. Once home, they would walk to the kitchen door rather than the stable and alert the mother of the house that they were home. That way, she could rescue and take care of her husband. Hopefully, the horses received a well deserved treat as a thanks for their consideration.

The Traditional Fall Horse Gathering

Iceland is a land of history. Many traditions are kept alive and revered today just like they were in the past. Every year, large herds of mares, foals and geldings are turned out in the highlands in order to develop street smarts and to enjoy freedom and plentiful grass. Bringing them back in the fall and returning them to the farms is a very special occasion and a major social event.

Although everyone was invited to the festivities in the old days, only the farmers, themselves, were allowed to be a part of the actual gathering of the horses. Today, things have changed, and several trekking companies are able to arrange riding tours where participants can enjoy the last, less tricky part of the roundup.

A couple of centuries after inhabiting the island, the Icelanders placed a ban on the import of live animals. This was done in order to prevent or at least halt the spread of the contagious diseases that were raising havoc in Europe. Because the ban has never been lifted, every horse born in Iceland, today, is guaranteed to have been absolutely purebred for more than 1000 years.

Over the centuries, the horses came to offer an additional bounty to the hard working farmers. Countless ship loads of unbroken horses were sent to the Scandinavian countries to be used by owners of small farms. Others were sent to the United States and Great Britain to work in the mines. The Danish military used them to haul cannons and one of the Danish Kings used several Icelandics as his favorite hunting mounts. Justin Morgan is rumored to have been an Icelandic and the Spotted Saddlebreds claim their breed has Icelandic Horse ancestors.

Because they were wild—brought from the range, directly onto the boats—they acquired a label of being stubborn, but strong. In Denmark, when big draft horses and their carts got stuck in the mire, Icelandic Horses were sent for because they could drag them out. Research has shown that Icelandic Horses can out-pull other breeds 1.7 times per pounds body weight.

Icelandic Horses have always been known for their gait distribution. Even today, they are the only breed of horses known to be ridden in all of the five basic gaits.

Today, a certain type and quality of Icelandic Horse gaits has become important in the show ring and on the trail. In the old days, however, all that mattered was the comfort of the rider safety, speed, and the horse's endurance. But even early on, the ability of the horse to choose between many gaits was essential. By changing his foot-fall to suit the irregularity of the terrain, he could travel safely at high speeds across rocks, tufts, and tussocks.

Walk and canter were frowned upon as being useless. Trot was too uncomfortable for the rider to be used except when the terrain was extraordinarily rough. Gallop was ridden always—and only—for a only couple of hundred meters just before arriving home. The purpose of that was to show off how much unused strength the horse still possessed.

Even early on, flying pace was considered the ultimate show off gait but it was ridden only over very short distances and only in front of spectators. From about 200 to 100 years ago hvalhop —not toelt —became the favored riding gait. Because the horse canters on the hind legs and toelts with his front ones, the gait is not only amazingly comfortable to ride but also very energy saving for both horse and rider.

Settling Iceland was not easy, nor was living there through the centuries. Not only was the climate difficult and the terrain rugged, but there were also natural disasters like volcanoes. One in the eighteen hundreds especially wreaked havoc. Indirectly, it killed 80% of all the livestock. Only between 3000 and 5000 horses were left, causing great concern about the potential repercussions of inbreeding. Fortunately, long term, the breed ultimately emerged from the disaster even stronger and more tractable than ever.

Then came the age of mechanization. It changed everything in Iceland as well as in the rest of the world. As other means of transportation became available, working horses were less needed and the interest in them plummeted everywhere. In Iceland, only a limited number of passionate die-hard horsemen carried on the riding tradition.

Although this could have been a disaster for the breed, it—long term—turned out to be just the opposite. Serious breeders began to emerge along with the first shows and evaluations. A very limited number of stallions and breeding mares were honored, registered, and awarded the prize of either first or second class.

Back then, you couldn't enter your breeding animals in a judging the way you do today. A governmental horse consultant was appointed. He traveled around the country visiting farms, looking at their horses and listening to tales of especially promising animals on neighboring farms. Wherever he went, he selected the breeding animals to be evaluated and honored as well as the riding horses that would be eligible to enter the newly established horse shows.

National Championships were scheduled for every four years and in between smaller shows were held in each of Iceland's geographical corners. Each region bred its own distinct horse type suited for the environment and the personality of the people living there.

The horses in the rugged east part of the island were especially hefty and strong of body and spirit. The horses in the north were elegant, light-footed, and light-hearted. The horses in the South where the land was flatter and the grass more abundant were heavier and more laid back. The characteristics of the horses in the west were a mix of the north and south.

At least up until the advent of Internet sales and other tantalizing ways of spending money, the Icelandic culture was about honor and prestige rather than lucre. Prominent horses were not for sale to the highest bidder the way they are today. They were sold by the breeder—as a special honor—to a horseman he found worthy. The same was true of the use of top stallions. Being forward enough to ask if you could buy someone's horse without being offered was considered a serious social blunder.

Each Landsmot was taken more seriously than the preceding one. Being selected to participate was an enormous honor. Spectating was a major social event —each time attended by about 10,000 individuals from all over the island.

Horses and riders showed their magic on a flat grassy field. Alcohol was abundant and onlookers watched from adjacent grassy slopes sitting on blankets.

It quickly became tradition for participants and spectators alike, to ride to Landsmot and camp together in a designated area. Except for any stallions to be judged, all horses—including the ones participating—were housed together in a giant pasture.

One of the most amazing and treasured memories of my life was standing on a hillside watching the enormous horse herds intermingling below. Considering that each of the countless riders attending the show probably had brought at least three horses, the number of assembled animals was gigantic.

Participating horse owners took their performance very seriously. Watching the five-gaited class while attending my first Landsmot, I was surprised that most of the riders showed only toelt and flying pace rather than all of the required gaits. Finally, I asked the friends,we had come to the show with what the reason for this was. To them, the answer was obvious. “Only the ones who have no chance of doing well show more than the two important gaits,” I was told. There would be no honor in winning if you had show more than that.

Stallion owners were known to take dramatic measures when their professional honor was threatened. After having spent a lifetime creating an incredibly wonderful herd, one breeder from the south lands was dissatisfied with his judging scores. As soon as he came home, he slaughtered not only his stallion, but every horse in his massive herd. To make matters worse—as much as everyone had wanted one of his offspring or the use of his stallion—he had only let go of two horses in all the years he had been breeding.

The first—a gelding—became the Landsmot flying pace race champion. The other—a beautiful gray mare—became ours. One of our friends—the regional breeding president—had convinced the breeder to allow us to add her to our herd in Denmark. Luckily, she not only had a few foals there, but she had many more in California after we brought our horses here.

Then, in the beginning of the nineteen-sixties, a whole new era began for the Icelandic Horse. Like so may other young Icelandic men, Gunnar Bjarnasson, attended university in Denmark. He was an avid horseman and could not help comparing his native horse to all the other breeds he encountered. "We need to make the Icelandic Horse a household

name all over the world, he decided. Once he returned to Iceland, he set to work. No one could have wished for a better ambassador for the horse. In league with the Icelandic Farmer's Association, he conspired to make his dream come true. Luck was with him in the shape of another volcano.

He filled a freighter with foals and alerted the German media to the foals' dire situation. "If they remained in Iceland, they would all be slaughtered," he announced. He forgot to mention that volcano or no volcano that was the fate every year of most Icelandic foals. The story got great news coverage and buyers were waiting in line to rescue these darling little creatures just as soon as the ship docked.

The first ship load became one of many. Everyone fell in love with the adorable little creatures and couldn't get enough of them. Soon a demand for adult family horses began. The Icelandic Horse movement spread like wildfire and quickly thereafter other countries followed in Germany's footsteps. In a matter of only a few years, 10,000 Icelandics had been imported to the small country of Denmark. National associations were started and shows and other group functions became a part of every day living. Everyone loved these personable, easy-going, terrain-going horses that brought groups of people together without the need for expensive stabling.

The Icelandic Horse movement spread especially fast in Denmark because—coincidentally—the Icelandic government had given the Danish Queen and her prince two gorgeous mares as a wedding present. The queen's Icelandic Horses made a good news story, especially when her sons—the young princes—regularly, were seen riding them around the public park surrounding the royal summer palace.

Danes are a down to earth people. They are far from star struck. They did not flock to immediately buy Icelandics because they now could be considered more than shaggy little ponies. It was media coverage that, once again, got the ball rolling and made people aware of the many possibilities of the new breed in town.

In 1967, a group of inner circle Icelandic Horse enthusiasts from 5 countries united in Switzerland and formed an international association called FEIF—Federation of European Icelandic Horse Friends. The countries were Iceland, Germany, Switzerland, Denmark and Austria. Today, Gunnar Bjarnnason's dream has come true. FEIF encompasses 22 nations and has over 80,000 members.

Gunnar dedicated his life to the Icelandic Horse. He worked tirelessly for many years in many other ways to fulfill his vision for the Icelandic Horse. He was the ideal horse ambassador. Without him and the many other passionate Icelandic Horse enthusiasts— in Iceland and abroad—not nearly so many people, internationally, would have had the joy of owning and enjoying this magical horse. Among the favorites of this group of people are Reynir Adelssteinsson, Siggi Sæmundsson, and Ingimar Sveinsson.

As more and more horses were exported from Iceland, horse shows became a more important factor in the continental Europe and—especially in Germany—money began to talk. The perceived market slowly became targeted towards show animals and as a result the breeding standards were directed towards show business rather than an attempt to breed the perfect pleasure horse.

The Eyes Are The Mirror Of The Soul

This development became a concern among those who treasured the original Icelandic Horse, and there was fear that the new show scenario would change Icelandic Horse breeding radically. And that some of the best, original, Icelandic Horse traits— like friendliness, street smarts, power, strength, endurance, light sure feet, and color diversity—would be lost in the process.

What made made matters even more controversial was that the Icelandic vision of the future horse and the German vision grew increasingly at odds.

SYNCHRONICITY!

The Icelanders preferred sure-footed, light-footed, light-hearted, elegant, comfortable horses with distinct Icelandic Horse heads. Front leg action was important but it needed to be the result of added drive from behind.

The Germans sought flash both in personality and action. They went for heavier, coarser horses in a more carriage horse type. Very high front leg action was imperative but not necessarily paired with drive from behind. Comfort and fun were not nearly as important as ostentation. American Saddlebreds were envied.

At one point, there was even a move to breed predominately black horses because of the illusion that black legs silhouetted against the sky would look as if they had higher lift than legs of other colors.

Fortunately—although obviously enticed—the Icelanders persevered and were not won over by German money. Overall, they steadfastly continued to create the type of show horse that reflected their personality— a delightful light-hearted, light-footed, agile, level-headed, street smart, and colorful friend.

Nonetheless, it was more than the Icelanders' steadfast belief in their own values that saved the day. The miracle that has not only kept all the valuable traits forefront in the breeding, but even improved upon them is a combination of the trekking business and the great increase in pleasure riding amongst the Icelandic population.

As tourism has evolved into an important part of Iceland's economy, horse trekking has become—if not the most popular—then one of the country's most popular tourist attractions. A large number of trekking businessesranging from major enterprises to mom and pop ventures—have evolved. Horsemen from all over the world flock to go on cross country rides ranging from several weeks long to just a short jaunt as a part of a tourist bus stop.

The Magic Of Gorgeous Hair

The increase in horse demand has obviously been a boon for the Icelandic Horse industry, but the truly magical part is that the trekking business needs can not be satisfied by show horse culls.

Ideal trekking horses need to be of a type very similar to the one the Icelandic farmers developed over 1100 years. Among the desired traits are being willing, enduring, strong, sturdy, sure-footed, street smart, and very comfortable to ride.

Trekking hoses must have a forgiving temperament that allows them to deal with and satisfy both newbies and experienced riders. Add the more modern preferences to the mix such as beauty, color, and abundant mane and tail. Then you have the new winner—the ideal pleasure horse

THE JOY OF
COLOR!
42

The Eye
Is The Mirror
Of The Soul

Imagine The Joy Of Riding Under the Midnight Sun!

California Dreaming!

As children, many of us delighted in Dick Francis' books about the Black Stallion. Absolutely nothing is as joyful as a brisk ride along the ocean and plunging into it.

Fortunately, the Icelandic Horse is at his very best as an amphibiant. He loves water as much as his riders do. And—once he has become familiar with it—shows little fear of it.

We Californians love water and considering the Pacific Coast, we have a quite a lot of it, but unlike in Iceland where streams, rivers, and coast-lines are everywhere, we generally have travel a tad before we can enjoy the experience. Nonetheless, there is no doubt the joy of the adventure makes the trailering worth it.

MONTANA
MEMORIES:

It's Fun That Makes The World Go Around!

Fun is the most important ingredient in success. This is true for both people and horses. Ultimate success requires endless effort. Without fun one can only go so far before burning out. Reward your horse's efforts rather than attempt to force him to do more than he feels up to.

Landsmot Is
Fun For All Ages!

There is—indeed—something very special about the Icelandic Horse.

I hope you have enjoyed browsing this book as much as I have enjoyed creating it.

Check out my current websites:

https:// EHaug.com, https://SharingMagicMoments.com
and https://ElisabethHaug.com

ONCE AGAIN, MAY THE HORSE BE WITH YOU!

www.ingramcontent.com/pod-product-compliance
Ingram Content Group UK Ltd.
Pitfield, Milton Keynes, MK11 3LW, UK
UKHW060120300726
14090UKWH00002B/278

* 9 7 9 8 7 3 5 3 1 4 5 1 6 *